Sally Festing

Meeting Places

Meeting Places
published in the United Kingdom in 2025
by Mica Press & Campanula Books

https://micapress.uk | contact@micapress.uk

ISBN 978-1-869848-41-5
Copyright © Sally Festing 2025

The right of Sally Festing to be identified as the author of this work has been asserted by her in accordance with the Copyright, Designs and Patents Act of 1988.

All rights reserved.

Acknowledgements

With thanks to the magazines and websites that have printed my work.

Acumen, Agenda, Ambit, Assent, Critical Quarterly, Coffee House, Dream Catcher, Envoi, Equinox, Fenland Poetry Journal, Frogmore, Ghost Furniture, Ink Sweat and Tears, Interpreter's House, Iota, London Grip, Links, LUPO, Magma, Mary Evans website, New Welsh Review, The North, Obsessed with Pipework, Orbis, Outposts, The New Statesman, The Poets' Republic, Poetry Nottingham, Poetry Review, Seam, The Shop, Smith's Knoll, SMOKE, Snakeskin, The Spectator, Stand, Staple, The Times, Under the Radar, Wild Court, The Wolf, Wordplay and "14".

Grateful thanks to the dedicated editors of five chapbooks,
The Hawthorn Press, Happen*Stance*, Fair Acre Press, The Knives, Forks and Spoons Press; to Oversteps Books for a first collection and Les Bell of Mica Press for this one.

Invaluable support has come from Moniza Alvi, Peter Wallis, my family and the Norwich Stanza.

'first and foremost thank you to the coast because without the coast how do we move from here to there' - Gboyega Odubanjo

'The journey matters – because it *is* the arrival.'- Iain McGilchrist

CONTENTS

1. The Swim
2. Local History
3. Echoes
4. ToadWoman
5. Cutting Runes in the Sand
6. Cartographica
8. Julian
9. An Old Japanese Notion
10. Windsong
12. Jenny tries to become a Kneeling Figure
13. The Right Angle
14. Stone Fish
15. Guest Room
16. Light Snow: Sleeping Place
17. Burning
18. Weeding
19. Digging
20. Their Prints
21. The Kaiser's Groom
22. Jottings
23. The Endurance of Chairs
24. Market Scene
25. The Question of Uncle Ian's Balance
26. The Talking Cure
27. A Poetry of Release
28. Looking for 'Man of Stones'
29. Tell-tale
30. Pried open for all the World to see
31. Cycladic Faces
32. Ill in Bed for a Year
33. VE Day
34. Hot Dog Sculpture
35. Out of Bounds
36. Gormley's Baby
37. Niagara Falls
38. Twenty years and I mourn
39. Cess Pit
40. MRI Scan with a Video
41. Widening the Sky
42. To the Lord God of Movement
45. Poems for My Daughter:
    - i. Transcontinental Connections
    - ii. Harriet's New Romance
    - iii. Harriet tells me She's Moving On
    - iv. The Tree of Knowledge

    v. All in your Mother's Mind
    vi. Missing my Daughter in the Modern Life Café
51. Hotel
52. The Mole
53. White Peacock in Bilbao
54. Touching is a kind of Kiss
55. The Couple
56. Trying to Unite the Parts of my Life
57. Mowing
58. Feasting
59. Memory upends
60. On not giving up
61. World is what you touch

THE SWIM

The pool's pure Hockney – cool,
sapphire and super-real.
Virginia creeper blots the retaining wall.

Roses and walnuts in the thorny burr
and great leaf-spattered trees.
A cat stretches in the grass, tumbles into its fur.

I'd like to go on filling space like that.
Be butterfly. Bird.
An acrobat.

But there are lengths to kill
between one hard edge and the other,
back and forward, breaststroke, crawl.

LOCAL HISTORY

This morning I took the Coasthopper from Burnham Overy Staithe
to Sheringham, had to run, boarded breathless.

The driver said 'next time put out your hand, the *George Vancouver*
stops for everyone! Our buses start from Lynn.

They've all got names, one's called *Black Shuck*
after the dog who spooks the coast.

Fanny Billingham was hung in Norwich.
Sylvia Townsend Warner rented Randall's folly on Salthouse beach.'

I moved closer, told the driver I'd met STW but fixed on roads,
she didn't care to stretch Coasthopper lore.

ECHOES

I remember early morning, dawn coming up
under dusky skies, beachcombing,
foraging for wood
                when marram stripped
my legs and stung. The hungry miles,
three of us running,
when toads sang and sun blinded our eyes.

I remember long afternoons
when heat shimmered
off the dunes, and hoppers gathered
in my hair, and a fox lay
                decomposing
in the sandhills beside its lair.

I remember beauty in wreckage –
waves breaking in a million endings
and spray on trinkets of glass.

I remember evenings
when a muted sun gave way to stars,
when I lived outside, cried like a night owl,
when bats' echolocation bounced the air,
and the sky, a darkish olive-green,
made an oversized chessboard of marsh
and sand that focused my mind
when stars came out.
When shadows closed in.

TOADWOMAN
after a sculpture by Germaine Richier

She's toad in the leap   she's about   to spin

toad   in her svelt skin's   perfect shine

in the slope of her back   plumped thighs

needing only   a slug to jog   her appetite

She's toad   in the feisty stretch   to the unknown

CUTTING RUNES IN THE SAND

It's what kids do.
What I did too
beside the slate-blue sea,
rituals of creation
when days were as long as the cockle path
threading through the saltings
to Scolt Head.

Every day with all our gear,
and several times
when the water bottle was left behind,
I took a barefoot run
on mud-cracked hexagons.

The days were long.
              There was so much,
            so much time.

'Look! I made a perfect sun.'

CARTOGRAPHICA
after Josh Danziger's Norfolk wall maps

Cross-stitch, back-stitch, chainstitch, hem –
lines stitch together where flatness

eventually corrugates to sand hills
through a patchwork of waterways and marsh

before hours of dark open fistfuls of stars.
From two small Burnhams

with lines full of spirit, layer upon layer
are deeply embedded in my body

and mind, the weave so heavy.
The map is flat although it's partly sea.

I no longer jump through sunlight
from marram-grassed dunes.

We're scared of waves engulfing us
and the world is running out of sand.

Great views from the top, boasts the Coastliner –
wrinkles that furrow my face

intricately woven, through cockle bights,
Deadman's Hole, Butchers Beach, the Nod.

My place is Overy (over-the-water), estuary
to the Burn. Lines entangle me

from Island into sea, lips through which tides
spit and gargle, metallic lips edged in sand.

This tiny harbour village has its myths,
the Island full of noises, terns, ring plover,

it's like a thousand ... instruments, kree-er,
yodelling t'lew, t'lew, persistent pic-a-pic.

Oyster-catchers congregate and nest.
There were three of us when we first came.

*How tall you've grown. Half-fare, remember,
bend your knees and they won't see.*

Lines begged us to swim – a little death,
and half sea-swallowed, we'd leap from

gun-metal, marram-clad dunes.
Another step stitches round the lips

like a necklace of ripples on the strand.
Percussion beckons me to dance, mapping

the future, inhabiting a different space each time.
The map's strewn with razors, tellinas, oysters, gapers, clams.

Wild rugosas, are they still there? I'm a dancing poet now,
choreographing creeks, an ancient woman of this land.

JULIAN,

there's a lost language between us.
I can't walk through it but like a cloud it stays in my mind,
circling round the differences that make me sad.
Here, I am almost nothing among tousled hedges
on the sea's edge, the calming marshes, the rawness
where I come to save myself.
I'm an early riser and early sleeper
aligned to the sun and moon – I watch the mornings
when light falls unsparing. Once, my fine grown grandson,
I dragged you out of bed with my fingernails the way
the cat grabs a teenage bunny from its burrow in the grip of its teeth,
a small violence the shock of which touched every part of you.
It strips my skin to think how you hunched like a target
and cried with your lungs and guts out of your own short past,
and wanted a parental hand to hold you firm.
Life was precarious
when there should have been small moments
you and I could fold carefully away.
Instead there's silence like an empty plate, or a parched pond,
and the house takes on a sense of absence. Sometimes
there's a lot of solitude in a grey head, although I like
to be in this peacefulness and hope you can learn
to love this place, its emergence out of the earth, to brace
the waves and walk in inhospitable winds.
You fly to hot haunts with heated swimming pools.
Here you're restless, and I feel your restlessness.
    How can I find words we both understand?

AN OLD JAPANESE NOTION
after Roger Ackling

The day is late, sun almost gone when bearing a magnifying glass, watching for every shift and slant of light, he scampers up a hill to catch the last of it, intense, becoming abstract, minimal. He feels the shade coming on. So much undone ... what if it thunders suddenly, what if it rains? He makes lines with sunlight, lines in dots that look like lines in books. The sky up there is his room. He's focusing rays with his glass in a steady hand, trapping them. How near or how far? Twisted inside him, tension pours into his glass. He can't let go, rays pass through, bend and concentrate, burn, then he moves forward; each line lots and lots of little circles, every one an image of the sun. Little suns, he's gripped by them, making perfect forms unaided by colour. Few of us will touch the landscape in this way. Here he goes, around the final corner, sky carves into him like knives of light. By sundown each shimmering line has bitten the surface, burnt, sunwild. He gets to the end his 'page' - a piece of driftwood, lolly sticks, clothes pegs, handles, knobs, anything catches his eye; back, and he starts again, the space between the lines precise. He's gauging the turning of the earth, the falling of the sap on slit bamboo. Transforming the ordinary, overlooked, discarded, saying place, saying season. Sometimes feathers and petals stuck on. The North Sea becomes his hunting ground. He bristles with energy, pins or elastic bands. Sunlight chivvied him until his light dimmed to trails of footprints, almost a script. What do his lines say? Secrets? Plainsong? Sunlight dived into his life like transparent threads of silk. He wanted power over them. An old Japanese notion says *to paint bamboo, one has first to become bamboo.*

WINDSONG

Like the geese she is on her way.
Launched on the tides' unspeakable rhythm,
she stretches wings, planes in a force three wind,
skims from the harbor through marsh to the sea.
In the darkness of water the tide sings its song
where water and music lean on the wind.

She was birthed on a jig, parameters fixed
with station molds like staves on a music score.
Apron, hog and transom composed her spine.
She would float, tack and run with the wind,
the intervals set her song.
Seagull shadows dazzled the boathouse,
their cries lured the builders' minds.

Outside a broken wind spread infinitely thin.
The world was sick. The village went early to bed,
the swallows and house martins were leaving,
but inside the boathouse planking went on.
Western red cedar was epoxy-resined, glass-sheathed,
varnished, then sanded smoother than skin.

Turned upright she was an eggshell,
a fragile girl whose fishy ribs (bulkheads)
would shoulder the gunwales.
Air tanks were slipped in, a hog for the mast.
Deck and foredeck were scarfed together,
thwarts and centerboard-case fitted, mast stepped.
The almost-ready-for-a-party-girl was trim –

fourteen foot six with the bowsprit,
lug-rig, and fast like boats of the past
built by Breton and Scottie fishermen
(sailed by them in their own rendering),
hollow mast, yard and boom. Work was paced
to the fling of sea on the slipway.

The boathouse was stuffed with dreams
and the village shared each paring,

honored the grain. *Windsong* was a channel,
a challenge, a hymn full of solos.
The song in her pattern and weave
converged in the builders' hands.
She's buoyant as mackerel, light like a tern.

Note: The first Windsong sailing dinghy, built during covid in 2021 was the prototype for what is now a classed design.

JENNY TRIES TO BECOME A KNEELING FIGURE
after F.E. McWilliam

She twists without toppling, hands behind head.
One elbow on her knee, the other raised –
a simulacrum?

Our gallery guide too hunkers down, arm curved.
Daylight, clear as water, filtering through
the huge interior.

He breaks the moment *Can't be done, the figure has no torso.*
Instead of heart, gut, lungs – a stretch of sun.
We're in the Sainsbury Centre, and she laughs,

an eleven-year old's big laugh, and it echoes.
The sculpture balances – bird on air,
or dipped to earth and nearly off again.

I still see my great-niece, arm curved round.
On her face
her will to fill what's missing.

THE RIGHT ANGLE
*after a cartoon portrait of Lord Reith,
Director General of the BBC 1927-38*

One hand on hip, toe pointing to the ground,
Sir John's all angles, all points of view.
He knows what he stood for –
his argument was sound. The masses
would be educated and entertained.

'If a person is *famous*, it is superfluous
to point out the fact. If he is not, it is a lie.
The word will not be used on the BBC.'

Conservative to his angled brows,
TV was anathema to him, art
not finance, was radio's aim,
a boon he gained by royal charter.

Every year his name's embalmed
by the smartest brains around.
I think Reith's six foot six into reality.
He winks back at me.

STONE FISH
from Ecclesiastes 1&3

The Sun
hasTes
tO
fiNd his
placE

as Full
rIvers sift
the Stones
they gatHer

GUEST ROOM

We keep this space for family and friends
who race the Atlantic in carbon-spitting planes,

whose nakedness wakes up unused sheets,
who cram the room with travel-bags, computers,

cards of pills and sprawls of swimming gear.
Their darkglass summer eyes multiply our lives.

In this room, a room that eats the setting sun,
there's a stillness to be filled.

Night is like wide water. Faces flicker.
Behind the window, black talks back

and there's an owl shrieks through
the strangeness of the time.

LIGHT SNOW: SLEEPING PLACE
Richard Long's Lapland, 1983

Was it spontaneous or did you plan
                              to roll
your dreams in the bedding, pack your rucksack

and place it with snowshoes under a tree
for the photograph – two shallow dents

shaping what the traveller feels in empty tundra,
like a dog who pees and paws the ground

before heading off. Printing a path across
the great white wall of silence.

Is there something about a patch of ground
that's honoured your body, makes it owned?

BURNING

after the labours of the month (February) carved in stone
on the Norman font in St Mary's Church, Burnham Deepdale

This is a spare month.
Bare winter beginning.
Often the easterly cuts to the quick.

A tumble of birds
toss patterns over the marsh.
Wild music in the sky.

The tower bells clash
and his eyes stream.
February drives him in.

Home from the field,
he banks the fire,
stretches his feet

across the flames.
Consumed by the red and yellow,
the falling log, the gathered ash,

aware (but barely) of crashing, spitting,
he imagines himself the child
and hears his mother's anger.

A terrible thing.
She's angry as the bloody morning,
or, under his skin, the frozen sea.

Note: Nicolaus Pevsner calls Burnham Deepdale's font
'A *very rare and interesting piece*'.

WEEDING
(June) Norman font in St Mary's Church, Burnham Deepdale

It's a dream that rushes out of him
as he weeds, out of mindless repetition,
this strange life, day after day, June-time
when he'd rather riddle mussels, wash whelks,
or row offshore in his matchstick boat
to follow a silver slick.
Rather catch with a net, bait, hook or basket.
He longs for the tug of a mackerel,
itches to slit the fish.

The sea is a lodestone.
He lusts for its fat green squeeze,
water bouncing beneath the wood,
oars dipping out and in and out
of its depths. That's when he dreams
of flesh and shell and bone. Some days,
for hours, he finds his face in the water's surface,
wanting not to be always the same.
To have this other life.

DIGGING
    (March) Norman font in St Mary's Church, Burnham Deepdale

Some things the font doesn't show.
The way he would walk out into the wind,
hear it sweep through the leaves, turn his face

to test the morning, dreading a change
in the weather, pull back his shoulders
and stand inside his skin. How, raw

in the chill of his strip of land, he blew
on the cracks in his hands, asking the spade's sharp edge
to take him back into the dark, where she bloomed

girlish beneath the covers, a chicken stink
in her dress, the straw still in her hair.
How willingly she raised her mouth to his.

He watched the old Brent geese
flop down on the last year's stubble
and spotted a marsh harrier hung in the sky.

When life was only brutal, he felt locked,
limited, just a wave slapping
across the Wash to the Lincoln coast.

Unable to shape the shingle of every day,
he squared up where he left off,
forcing his heel down, so his blade

sliced through seeded weeds
almost without resistance, pushing in
among the roots. This stone can't show

how he dug as Adam dug away his sins,
expanding his ribs as the year broke from the earth.
Already it was March, and Spring.

THEIR PRINTS

Moths, ghosts, my house is full of them.
I live with waves of silence but their lives
roar enormous through my rooms -
hung on walls, stuffed in bookcases, leaking
from wounded suitcases tied with string.

It rained last night, and the dead came down
with the drops - to gather where the land is flat
and windblown. The quiet stores their smiles.
I press my fingers where theirs have been, thread
words to tumble them back, talking, arguing.

THE KAISER'S GROOM
*In 1853 my great grandfather made a journey across
the BalticSea to escort a temperamental racehorse.*

He stands on deck, gaping at the creature,
high and golden against the mast
before lowering it
through the hatch into the dark ship's hull.

He stops,
fears and longings held
in a skein. *Leicht leicht!*
It's unreal – the hour's brilliance,

a sling round the belly,
spread legs
dangling his future.

JOTTINGS
after Charles Richter (1867-1946), founder, Bath Cabinet-Makers

My father's father, sighs into his notebook.
Pencil held against clipped moustache,
his sighs fall among fragments of Nietzsche,
drafts of plays
and furniture designs.

He wants to discover what he doesn't know,
wants his inwardness to flow from his hand.
Straight lines keep the heart in check.
Curved lines shape his art.
What really counts is the grain.

Landscape skips and dives like an eyelid's flicker.
He tries to let the moment open,
to shake off a shrill note
but his mind keeps leaping as his pencil riffs.
Get to the root of it, says the train.

Gold medals roll in, taking rest is a forgotten flower.
Concentrating as the train draws in,
he shifts between striving and self-reproach.
I see his elegant script break into runs –
regret, yearning.

Note: In the 1920s B.C-M became the second largest furniture maker in the UK.

THE ENDURANCE OF CHAIRS

Imagine the chain of love behind curved oak arms
and backs; how wood first slipped beneath the joiner's
hands as he spat and whistled a tune,

overalls, cloth cap. How he steamed to bend
his smoker's bows, shavings thick as willow leaves,
air choked with dust (an early death).

We've sat on them and been happy.
We've stood on them to hang glitter,
settled the tabby on each seat at night.

We've gentrified them in plum-hued suede.
They've moved with us, seen our children leave,
will probably honour our end.

MARKET SCENE
Aunt Eone's pastel

She's mapping in sunshades
open across her sketch
like harvest moons, raising such hopes
they create little throbs inside her.
She'll call it *Étaples Market*
when she dares to colour it.

There's a vertical strip of sky between
blocks of building, vivid behind the throb
of bartering. Banks of food for sale,
thrusting hawkers, aproned women
in small white caps and widow's weeds –
(the endless grief of World War I).

Above all, there's her tutor,
whose presence brings the very soul
of market closer.
For a moment her yearning for him
comes on like madness.
Like jumping off her moons

onto the sun. The next move matters,
let's say it's a high cliff leap.
She rests her chalk.
Sighs. Reaches to touch the sky.
This buoyant June
she could kiss a stranger.

Note: Eone's tutor took her for a brief trip to Paris. Her father was so angry at this that she tried to commit suicide. Hauled from the sea, she developed schizophrenia, and never recovered.

THE QUESTION OF UNCLE IAN'S BALANCE

i.
He was stuck   on a tightrope
under   huge unleafy trees

Weeping for his sister   He looked down
but he wobbled   god he wobbled

Family were all   shattered
by her shattering   No one guessed

the wretchedness   he buried in his head
the sting   of what

He didn't admit   his barefoot steps
along the lines   the damage they carried

ii.

War
    and the whole earth cracked.
he wanted a trigger to pull.

He tipped. He lost his hair.
The trees were his hair whipped stiff.

Like a blind white larva that couldn't pupate,
he was breakable but wouldn't give in.

No one knew how madly he gambled.
HeeHH tried to walk on his hands.

Note: Ian had shown signs of instability since childhood. With the stress of war on the family business, he too developed schizophrenia.

THE TALKING CURE

Cool as an eel
he slipped between syllables,

dissected text.
Theories sprouted like flowering trees.

The ritual was fixed.

Berggasse 19

to and fro on the steps *ding-dong*.

Talk. Talk – unmentionable things –
listening, he wrote it down.

They must understand
the nakedness of dreams.

Taming the animal passions wasn't easy.
It wasn't sin,

it was unmapped landscape

A POETRY OF RELEASE
after WS Graham

My father's efforts ran unhindered as the rain.
Those dearest to him from childhood

gone, he thought grief a gift he should earn.
There's relatively little words can do for grief

but what else did he have?
There were, he knew, huge worlds to explore,
                                            to share.

*

Let this poem be a still thing, a mountain
constructed from glass. I begin with

the ghost of an intension which blasts itself
to nurture a new collision.

Perhaps the shape of us – the wreckage,
the shame and the dance – is in our language.

Note: After Derek Richter's second sibling developed schizophrenia, he became a noted neuropsychiatrist.

LOOKING FOR 'MAN OF STONES'
Laurence Edwards 2019

'Off the path
    follow the wood
        my dog always barks at him.'

There,
    emerging from the lake
        a braced body labours

through
    every shape
        his burdens make

open to blizzards
    hurricanes
        blinding rain –

resolute among nettles
    fading Rose Bay
        maples bindweed oaks and willows

yet he connects
    sticks and stones
        hung from his neck like trophies.

Just
    think
        what he shoulders

TELL-TALE

My first day home from boarding school
she sat us among the heirlooms
blinking uncomfortably
as bats in daylight.

Her disclosure concerned our father
and rather than turn traitor
I didn't take it in.

She might have said
It's an apocalypse
the life you know is over.

Posh furniture made everything go numb.
If we'd sat on the terrace
I'd have chopped off
my ears' confusion.

'PRIED OPEN FOR ALL THE WORLD TO SEE'

Poets tell what once they locked in their heads.
Mother called it getting things off your chest
and she didn't refer to clothes, she meant chunks
of psychic landscape. Cliffhangers like the time
you tried suicide or genuflexed to God in clouds of gloom.
How you forced baby sister to gobble blackberries,
had her lick sick from her lips. How you argued with
Dad's woman at the top of your voice, needling him.
Oodles of stuff whirrs in the parts we kept PRIVATE.

Note: Title from Berryman

CYCLADIC FACES

Heads tilted back, feet pointed down
they could have run on sand and left no trace.
But love, you understand, goes on and on,
each holds its secrets in a pale flat face.

They could have run on sand and left no trace.
Cycladic images possess my mind,
each holds its secrets in a pale flat face,
arms folded on its chest, like you, father, friend.

Cycladic images possess my mind,
then you in your hospital bed, a deity,
arms folded on your chest, father, friend,
stoic and timeless as stone's eternity.

You in your caring bed a deity,
head tilted back, feet pointed down,
stoic and timeless as stone's eternity.
while love, you understand, goes on and on –

Note: My father died in Horton Hospital, 1995.

ILL IN BED FOR A YEAR

I smooth out Roses Chocolate wrappers,
raise them to my eyes, squint
through transparent film – yellow is laburnum;
green, glades and pools;
pink, flurries of cherry-blossom;
purple, star-shot night. There's bluest
blue, compared to which
all other skies seem faint-hearted.

Sweet papers are my private screen.
No usher's torch. No popcorn,
no smoke-wreathed gloom.
Only imagination's sweetness.
Am I the person I've always been?

VE DAY

I hold a finger to my chin. Flowers bind my hair. White tablecloths stretch endless invitation. Flags fly. Plum trees pink the pavements and I'm stumbling into sun, brother a sweep, sister a fairy. I'm tall for my age, too tall for a wand. A nurse perhaps? (there are several nurses) but 'flower-girl'? I'd rather be a levitating angel, one finger on my chin. And why does everyone kill everyone? What about blackouts? sirens? Have I imagined riding the weir in my Micky Mouse gas mask, snorkelling with its rubber snout when warships plough the Cam – gunning down punts, tossing up courting couples as ducks skidaddle on the puckered surface and Nurse guards sister in a tankish tasselled pram. Think how night times, blinds down, tomcats slink the garden, invade my dreams. How soldiers march past, rifles raised, so I rock until I scream. War-to-end-wars, what does this mean? I'm watching the photographer, it's before I tangle in the snares of time. My mind's still clean. Before and after follow each other and light slips away each day. There's a tiny jester, a scowling girl in stars and stripes, a boy in fanciful headgear. Little red riding hood. A queen. None of them smiles. What do I know about world domination? Hitler's aim? Millions killed. Millions more like the mouth-organ man who doesn't have legs and plays by the kissing gate to the meadows. Like others with crutches I see in trains. How many's a million really?

Note: Street Party in Selwyn Road, Cambridge, 8 May 1945

HOT DOG SCULPTURE
after Colin Self

Wow what a bite for those who dare
but sexy metres black as nite have a charred look
and Self's slick split flavour

is sandwiched fast
It was nineteen sixty fourabouts and he was wary of nuclear war
Imagine the polyester resin aftermath

OUT OF BOUNDS
For Sale. The Sunday Times displays
a honey-coloured pile.

Midnight I led illicit troops onto the roof.
Later, summoned to the Head's dreadful study,
I paid for sins.

Leo, Regent, Stucco, Princess, Cornflower –
our dormitory windows framed the pampas
pluming in new-crushed grass.

Mozart spilled through the Italian Gardens,
our songs shuddered the chandeliers,
cartwheels hardened lawns beneath the portico.

Sunday afternoons I lay behind the 15th century church
with a book and the lakeside view.
Walking round that lake. Did it help me escape

the palace where our fathers paid so handsomely
to place our promise in someone else's hands
or was it the appeal of out of bounds?

Once a cormorant flew to the lake.
It was under a long time searching for fish.
I knew what it meant to find myself lost

in a blear of the flow. The building isn't gold,
it's Portland stone. We wore grey hats to match.
And grey rain washed my long hikes past the boathouse.

GORMLEY'S BABY

Crouched in the courtyard
where feet meet stone. New-born,
life-size, this tiny bomb,
sucked in air. *Iron Baby*
snug on the ground, was lost
in the scale of things.

Sea-creature, peach, pumpkin,
sugar plum – drupelike, fleshed,
dreaming of the breast as she nestled.
Chocolate without a wrapper,
she wanted skin to touch her own.

Geometry hovered over her,
and Friends waited for friends.
Distances are fixed
and our planet's core is iron.
The years walk before her,
her head will be forested.

Note: Antony Gormley's sculpture was shown in the Royal Academy courtyard in November 2020.

NIAGARA FALLS
for Alice

'Only a small cut in your eye. You stay awake throughout.' A rush of water, waterfall, downpour loud and sheer, cascade like Niagara where I travelled in a Hillman, nursing number one. I didn't know she was going to leave so soon.

'Blink for me' my consultant says. 'You mustn't move. We use very sharp tools.' The big black ultrasound stands statuesque to pound a sequence of his devising with geometries of flashing light. Like a photographer wild with zoom, he ships each message through his fingertips, sucking the small dead fish from my eye, dissolving it like a memory, leaving its sheath behind.

I focus on the moment of depletion, my eye enormous and still, a bloated sleeping seal. Water swills. He pops a stranger in. And here's more water, Niagara sheets my cheek, pouring down the walls of my mind.

Bless technology, I've an eye to weep, and my seeing lens comprehends that some leave sooner than you want them to. Distance distorts. I hold my child close, the missing one.

TWENTY YEARS AND I MOURN
i.m. Alice

Dear three-month chubby babe I'm floating on air, your fingers in the petal
of your mouth breathing lightly as a gull, the almost-smile, a stillness
with your body in my hands. I weep for you Alice, you feel so close.
You lie above me, inside me, a bird, a moth, a plane. You kicked your legs,
you are mischief, shooting them beyond my hands where space opens out

*

You're higher than me, unafraid, because my two hands hold you tight.
My glow-stick, coloured gleams, or Barlach's hovering angel bathed
in light. There's stillness with your body in my hands while time stretches,
five, ten, twenty years. This image lies inside me, your tunes, your skimming
sail, memories your dried clay saves – the art you'll leave behind.

*

I weep for you Alice, you feel so close, a constant sorrow,
a wandering pain when you're practising the cello, your arms consumed
by the flow of your bow. We listen to Elgar with Jacqueline Dupré, the
suffering, sighing, fast crescendo, fortissimo's moon-drenched melody, its rhythm
the noise of an ocean, the world disappearing at the end.

*

In the pulse of sea, your song is sailing a twelve-foot Topper. You are a bird,
a moth, a plane's contrail, behind you the varnish of separated water
is wedded once again. Water is new space, water is safe, provides you
with waves of calm; tacking, you're assured of its mass. So many corners.
A rush of wind, you're a fish swimming, a swallow turning in mid-air.

*

But everyman is made of clay, and soon it's your inner sun, layer upon
layer in the building before a pot is won. Each is a drama, and you at its centre
pattern some with lines, straight or wavy like your gold-brown hair.
There are five still apples in your picture, two of them, peeled, expose
tender skin, their green and purple set you free to dream.

*

You lie above me, inside me, dear three-month chubby babe, the distance
between us closes again. Silently a bird flies through you, nests in the flower
of your ceramics. Colour, line and space move through you. A pot topples,
destroys itself – going, going, gone. You're flying, not the bird, it's you
dragging hunger from the sky.

CESS PIT

With all the rain our great provider wished
upon us this long winter,
a brick-lined pit dug umpteen years ago
(I had no inkling it was there) - its boards fell in.

More than six foot wide, more than eight foot
down. The shock.
The fear of falling into piss, shit,
bone-eating worms.

My need to fill the wretched thing.
How to bury a year
of crumbling certainties?

Last night North Norfolk's moon went carnival,
its light so stark, it would have lit
that gap, that chasm
in the dark -

a hole that might have gone on swallowing
flower beds, deer-molested shrubs
and lawn - if the builder hadn't traipsed

to and fro, barrow after barrow, tipped in rubble
on a bitter day, to fill it.
Three truckloads he stomped down.
We thought the grass would never grow again.

The unveiled moon was firm,
repeating:
'You move on.'

MRI SCAN WITH A VIDEO

I'm trying to erase myself, trying on a costume, nothing metallic - no bra, watch, hearing aids, tattoos, implants. In this tunnel roofing, a wood, mountains, lake; birds fly left, clouds move right, slither in and out of focus, magnetic, resonant, disappear and reappear. A glib presentation but I can keep singing while staring into the void - everything connected, fear quiet in the lake of my heart through colourless miles of air. Like thoughts, like film, over and over, my guiding spirit floats across the sky. The lake with its tiny island calms. Voice intersperses imaging; *the next scan is three minutes ... the next scan*

Put that wood, savage and dark and dense in your pocket; trapped by condition, lock it. Corroborate. Listen. Try to repeat, it's mesmeric; mallow, ox-eye daisy, borage, bird's foot trefoil. Do I contradict myself, straddle a divide or connect? Is this revelation or erasure? Shimmer the poem in between, following its voice. Close my eyes a minute and I could be lost. Is it a trap? Try to laugh. Pretend it won't be downhill until the end. Listen to the fell, its swirl of falling bodies. Your poem is resistance, like Blake shows Dante, hell-bound, battling that dark slope of the brain.

WIDENING THE SKY

i

When my daughter married a Tamil
his mother went dumb –

there is a close-up of her beating
her heart against a wall.

ii

My son has an Asian lover
who dances, rattling the rain.

Same old story, families
trip over their tongues.

iii

Water spits from silted drains
as the monsoon reproves

iv

until grandchildren –
their peppercorn eyes.

TO THE LORD GOD OF MOVEMENT:
Visit to my Granddaughters in Brooklyn

i.
I'm globe-hopping, I'm wrapped in stars,
black and gold trainers.
Note-book, novel,
I am myself.

ii.
First house martin yesterday over the garden,
its flight my celebration.

Hi Jessica, it's Anna. I'm in the Departure Lounge.
Ex-Vasar executive taps her heel.
Close my eyes, allow the world to glaze.

Hi George, it's Anna.
In Economy, one is herded.
Close eyes, hear the bleat of lambs.

Hello Lorna, Hi ...

In an emergency, pull only one of the red tabs.
It is important that you do not inflate your vest until ...

iii.
Like a mountain goat, I make for my lodging.
Smells of spices, garbage,
Hispanic corners, Arab shops.
Black and gold trainers pitter-pattering
on grey stone flags and brown stone houses.

My granddaughters wear trappings from Sri Lanka,
gold in their hair, on their throats, arms, foreheads.
Glamour as large as a bride in her bath.
And after the tight warm hugs,
I start to sing.

iv.
Grand Central Park, a boating lake;
elder sister dreams.
Water is her servant,
swamps her world, her mind.

Prince Charming kisses the Barbie doll,
Darling I am yours.
Sleek as a seal with apple breasts,
Younger sister swoons.

A boat rows past
splashing the water's sky.
She drifts like a pink pink cloud.
Long day in July.

v.
Piped music flares to a raz of tulips,
stink of horse piss,
tourist carriages,
kids on scooters, roller skaters.

An old woman with a coke-can.
Up her straw roar
public sculpture, odours, petals.
The moment rises;   vanishes
in leaf-filtered sun.

vi.
Rain through waves of Brooklyn leaves,
picnic tables sad and rained on.
I lie in my 80 dollar a nighter
reading Jackie Kay.
I think of the girls' long weedy hair
within this same embrace,
same rattle and race of water
shed on a shuttle of spread umbrellas;
making the same refrain.
I'll lift them in my arms.

However hard I try,
I can never get close enough.
Today's today; it may not come again.

vii.
I could have dreamed the trip.
Dreamed morning tea at five.
That I skipped through tall brown lamp-lit streets
alive to the small naked bodies of next year's women
in last night's bath.

POEMS FOR MY DAUGHTER

    i.   Transcontinental Connections

Four pm. and you've gone.
Larky sun. Garden bursting.
A heron has gobbled the last flash
from the pond, fledgling in the rambler
                                is set to fly.

*

Dithery, I bake a cake,
        sifting into your skyscraper office,
your brave smile, sucked fingers
as you press on, wait
for the telephone. Waiting is worse
than disappointment. Will they accept
your application?
Your pain is also mine.
        Remember,
still at school you asked five friends
or was it six, to play? One by one they all
cried off, except Milly. She turned up
true as a wet stone's shine.

*

Next time, you'll flop your mane.
Arm in arm, we'll taste the garden.
You'll flick your hand among waterlilies,
laugh 'Let's buy more goldfish.'

ii.   New Romance

She's with her professor boyfriend, sipping wine
in a fancy hotel, hearing how his arms
once enclosed, if not every woman in LA,
a fair number of them. One day,
close to his former home, the mountain
silence almost overwhelmed them –
trees blackened by a fire,
a hawk soaring in the sky.

Later, they walked across a headland,
descended the bluffs and there was a beach,
wide, clean, and almost deserted. She swam
through more than a year since they met,
his wives and lovers cramming the landscape.

He's always been open, she knows he's
a man with a past. When they blast rock
from the car (he has a headful of song),
when she wakes in his embrace, or stands
watching the cormorants preen their wings,
she's a breaker of any sea.

iii.　Harriet tells me She's Moving On

Two days on the road
through an Autumn dazzle,
crunching chocolate coffee beans.
In between he sings to Dylan, Clapton, Springsteen,
Beach Boys and the Beatles. My hand on his lap
when he drives, his hand on mine when we swap
round until who is who
                        isn't all that clear.
Musing through the options for my ring
we're checking out how far we've come,
new life, blue skies, moving on.

New life. Blue skies. Moving on.
We're checking out how far we've come.
Musing through the options for my ring,
now that who is who
                        isn't all that clear. His hand
on my lap as I drive, mine on his when we swap
round, singing to the Beatles, Beach Boys, Springsteen,
Clapton and Bob Dylan. In between
we're crunching chocolate-covered coffee beans
through a Autumn dazzle
on the road again. Two days we'll be home.

iv.   The Tree of Knowledge

You say, you saw a slinky black racer curled in the Walters Viburnum.
Serpent, serpent, slithering a fissure. Not venomous, but cornered
it strikes sharp and deep. Coluber constrictor priapus perhaps?
America has its monsters, this isn't one.

Days race by and you're what? Five hours away by sky, five hours in time.
What does my longing mean?

Here there's a fearful onshore breeze – God's revenge for terrible things?
What sin must I atone for? Or is it always the other who's the ecodenier,
woman-decrier, trigger-happy, nationalist, racist?

You say you almost watered the snake, had a shock because it blended
with the leaves, shook its tail as if to scare a predator. Who's afraid of who?

Youtube. I watch a racer shake its tail. Eve, and panic in the apple tree.

v.   All in your Mother's Mind
> *10.5 million children lost a parent or caregiver because of Covid.*
> Washington Post

I'll wish away your hose burden, the chiggers, grumps.
Wish you water for the live oak, three cocoplums
and four lusty lyonias.
For your huge life wrapped around work and garden.

I'll frighten the alligators that lie in your path in Barr Hammock.
Maybe lure them off with oranges.
Or was it crocodiles that eat oranges? *

It's like dictators take a holiday from poisoning their rivals.
Like the cost of funerals hasn't risen above inflation.
Like numbers in intensive care are not ... not.
How quickly public life encroaches on all we hold dear.

Harriet, it's like being with you,
watching you in a hot-tub watching through binoculars
a red-shouldered hawk.

Something tells me it's always like this –
swimming the big river until it shrivels into a pool.
We're such fools to complain!

Note: Katherine Mansfield, short story, *Poison*.

vi.   Missing My Daughter in the Modern Life Café
*The number of deaths from Covid-19 in the UK
exceeds 50,000. BBC News*

Beyond the twenty-foot glass wall,
Philip King's scarlet sun embraces the lawn.

I can squint through roots implied by latticework
of grassgreen steel, to beech, cedar, larch and yellow limes.

Students jog past, sometimes couples.
Cyclists press wheels into the ground.

If I reach deep in the trees, I'll access dreams –
your head of hair across my arm's

a hug of sun. But dreams unhinge,
delude me with their childhood roots.

The painted sculpture defines space between sun
and earth. Trouble is I want you with me

inside the high glass wall to share *Sun's Roots*.
I reach out my hand.

HOTEL

In our high-up room
I'd like to make you fall in love with me
all over again,
your hands on me, young
in the soft shush of air conditioning.

Cornflower sky;
silent forms descend from the arch
under the church of Austros Varty.
Nuns slip to and fro like dominoes,
prostrate themselves in the street.

I arrange myself,
the daintiest dish in Vilneus,
naked as the fish we ate last night,
and gauzy beside the river,
I'll flash my scales
until you're powerless.

THE MOLE

Seborreic keratosis. It's almost a shame
to lose what looks like grainy skin

on the surface of my thigh. A blemish
I don't much dwell on now bikini days

have gone. It does no harm
and once upon a time, before you grew blind

in one eye, the other so light-sensitive
it craves perpetual hibernation,

before rheumatics made a mockery
of one hand, I remember a touch so full

of lust and love, it blasted me
far over the earth.

WHITE PEACOCK IN BILBAO

He amourettes from time to time, peers bill to bill
at another male, his snowy spill hopelessly bridal.

Desirous as Joseph Beuys' bird women, feather eyes
and downy hair, their nipples sprouting wings.

Or Emily Dickinson behind her door,
breaking words apart in small slant flights.

TOUCHING IS A KIND OF KISS

If his touching is a kind of kiss
and kiss is touch, is it a synonym
that somersaults me in, or is it him
in me? If so, a kiss is fathomless.

Teasingly he flicks my ribs, my arm.
Kiss, kiss, I wake to be undone.
Soon I'm in red alert. Unruly sun!
High time to switch off the alarm.

If playing footie is a sip of snow,
a quick flurry suggesting fire below
a blanket, flakes float pianissimo.
So does his tongue. Even my toenails know.

A touch is kiss is touch, like sky and sun.
Either would ache without the other one.

THE COUPLE
after the sculpture by Germaine Richier

They sound each other, bounce off the other,
feet off the ground. In violent
union, they're holding hands –
their legs attenuated, bodies distended,
equilibrium precarious. He sings
to bind him to the earth, brings her myths,
wakes a pageant of forms
beyond the reaches of her bones.

Beyond the reaches of her bones,
he wakes a pageant of forms,
sings to bind him to the earth, brings her myths.
Their equilibrium is precarious,
bodies distended, legs attenuated.
They're holding hands in a union
that's violent. Feet off the ground,
they bounce off each other, each sounds the other.

TRYING TO UNITE THE PARTS OF MY LIFE

Lightly the stylus danced,
Ol' Man River. Running river.
Vibrations shake me.
Their languor carries me elsewhere,
A'm *scared of dyin ... /He must know sumpin'/*
But don't say nuthin'.../ He jes keeps rollin along.'
Me too, scared. Not dying,
but just not doing, so tangles remain uncombed.

Dad's still chasing the three of us.
I'm screaming my head off as I run.
He follows in deepening darkness,
rolled newspaper, eggs us on.
We run like scarves, like rivers,
round the house and ever after ...
Hypnotized by family drive,
I rotate in grooves of vinyl 45s.

August is yellow. Emoji month,
unsmiling, because the ocean's fever
has reached a record once again.
August is overtaking, inside, outside – tourists
with their wheelies and their phones,
like hopscotching the pavement eighty years ago.

A summer torrent flashes through leaves,
solid sheets on paving slabs, in gutters, blocking drains.
There's pain because my day was planned
and here's me trapped inside my wigwam.
Me needing to find the self lost
in unpropitious times,
to find words –
the tune that nags 'go on'.

Deluge thunders my umbrella
like a first night at the Proms.
We must connect like atoms,
be marbles whizzing round,
waves of water dancing on a pond.
Trying to unite parts of life,
I notice the birch tree spreading
like Adams' *Doctor Atomic* when Gerald Finley sings.

MOWING
(July) Norman font in St Mary's Church, Burnham Deepdale

What's in his mind when he adjusts his grip,
angles the cutting edge to accommodate
the dip and swell of the ground, swings the curved shaft?
The sward falls, the years spread around
and he's dancing with this lover in his arms.
But when he turns, there's only a swallow
set on an unforgettable journey.

Does he think about the saint's miracles
or what the priest says about struggle and forgiveness?
It's the next world that counts. The fire of hell,
that frightens him. Can he adjust to the unknown?
Can he face bad luck? He ends up scared
which way to turn. July swirls though his head.
The sea swells and sucks.

FEASTING

(December) Norman font in St Mary's Church, Burnham Deepdale

Flat plates, bowl, mead, stick of bread.
Christmas of course, with four squeezed
round the table, neighbours, friends.
Skinny men, their beards pointed silver, enjoying
the unmoored speech, the camaraderie.

Analogues of us, without frills,
they clean the shells of their little boats
and tuck them into the diddering[1] marsh.
Some are poets, and solitary,
though conviviality is at the heart of life.

Secretly, each wants someone else
who suffers, someone alternately happy
and wretched, like them. Their hearts
don't grow old, nor do the problems fade.
Life runs on beneath acres of sky.

Note: 'Diddering is a Norfolk word meaning to rattle or shiver.

MEMORY UPENDS

Nurse's grip is fondling.
Vet's grip is clawless.
Canula inserted, needle ready –
You want me to do this? It's very quick.
Eyes in cat's tabby face
lose sight of the sky.

On the allotment you dig deep,
through stony ground.
I carry him like a child in a sling.
Headfirst he drops in.
Furred engagement with dark space.
Diamond eyes where we won't plant anything.

    We wait for the flap's clatter,
    the contour of cat,
    wave of his tail
    as he sways towards us.
    Waiting coils inside our minds,
    licks its paws.

ON NOT GIVING UP
after Peter Dale

Your fear of falling, my need to be free.
Your bent frame fixed square
on the pot-holes. Electric wheels whirling air
scarcely rebut our southwesterly.

The allotment's not far.
You've the handlebars. Cling.
Blasts that scatter birds on the wing
won't fell a helmeted star.

WORLD IS WHAT YOU TOUCH

We no longer hold hands
because you need a walking-stick to stand.
Instead we slip together in the afternoon, stretch
across the double-bed we don't use at night
now you're restless –
I lie fingers on your arm,
toes against your skinny tibia
and it's enough through seaweed feet
to slither deep
not into sleep but another world.

My skin is listening to a familiar haunting,
little songs tuned to my body,
a pulse of openings and closings
anchored where oceans form and dissolve
scatter and gather,
changing and remaining the same.
I peer at the elemental
extraordinariness of lying here, chilly-boned –
a flame passing through
to do with all I breathe and am.

www.ingramcontent.com/pod-product-compliance
Lightning Source LLC
Chambersburg PA
CBHW061235070526
44584CB00030B/4128